2019 ROMAN REPLIES & CLSA ADVISORY OPINIONS

SR. SHARON A. EUART, RSM, JCD
EDITOR, ROMAN REPLIES

VERY REV. PATRICK COONEY, OSB, JCL
REV. MSGR. MICHAEL A. SOUCKAR, JCD
EDITORS, ADVISORY OPINIONS

Canon Law Society of America

ISBN 978-1-932208-53-5
ISSN 1543-4230
SAN 237-6296

Unless otherwise noted, all canons quoted are from the *Code of Canon Law, Latin-English Edition* (Washington, DC: Canon Law Society of America, 2012) and the *Code of Canons of the Eastern Churches, Latin-English Edition* (Washington, DC: Canon Law Society of America, 2002).

Printed in the United States of America.

Canon Law Society of America
415 Michigan Avenue NE
Suite 101
Washington, DC 20017-4502

Table Of Contents

FOREWORD

The Canon Law Society of America (CLSA) publishes annually *Roman Replies and CLSA Advisory Opinions* for canonists and those seeking a clearer understanding of the *praxis legis* of the Catholic Church. The combination of these two services, begun in 1984, continues to serve as useful resources for those involved in the application of canonical discipline.

The compilation of materials for *Roman Replies 2019* was guided by Sister Sharon A. Euart, RSM, Chair of the CLSA Publications Advisory Board. The collection of entries in this issue, when viewed in conjunction with previous volumes, assists the reader both in understanding recent developments in the law and in identifying current trends in the praxis of the Roman Curia.

The selection, editing, and assembly of opinions for *CLSA Advisory Opinions 2019* were provided by Reverend Patrick Cooney, OSB, and Monsignor Michael A. Souckar. The topics addressed in the opinions reflect a variety of canonical issues and demonstrate the scope of canonical expertise and reflection by members of the Society. Editorial assistance was provided by the CLSA Administrative Office.

Roman Replies and CLSA Advisory Opinions that are out-of-print are available electronically on the CLSA website (www.clsa.org). As an additional resource, the CLSA Advisory Opinion Online Index includes all published opinions, grouped by canon number on the CLSA website.

The CLSA provides this series as a professional resource. Care should be taken in considering the relative weight of the materials found in this publication. The principles for canonical interpretation (*CIC* cc. 16-19 and *CCEO* cc. 1498-1501) serve as guides in considering the contents of this volume.

Roman Replies

Introductory Note

The following is the editorial policy of Roman Replies. The policy, as well as the source of these materials, was first described in the 1984 edition and, with some modifications, has been in effect since that time.

Each year members of the Canon Law Society of America are invited to submit recent replies from the various dicasteries of the Holy See which might be of interest to the Society's members and the wider church. Judicial vicars, chancellors, vicars general, major superiors of institutes of consecrated life and societies of apostolic life in the United States, and professors of canon law are encouraged and asked to submit material for this important publication.

Contributions from members of the Society resident in other countries or members of other canon law societies are always most welcome. All contributors receive a complimentary copy of the volume.

Certain editorial principles determine the selection of documents for this publication. First, in general, entries which have already appeared in various canonical journals would not normally be repeated here. An exception is the publication of an official English translation of documents which already has been published in an unofficial translation. Second, documents which merely restate something published earlier with no added nuances or changes are not normally included. Third, documents that concern a matter not yet resolved by the Roman dicasteries are held for future publication in the hope that the entire matter may be fully reported when the question or controversy has been resolved. Finally, all details of names and places are changed to protect confidentiality, unless otherwise specified by the submitting individual.

A special note of thanks to all those who have submitted texts, helped with translations and who otherwise contributed to this 2019 edition. It is our hope that this volume continues to be a service to all who work in the ministry of justice in the Church.

Contributions may be sent to:

Canon Law Society of America
415 Michigan Avenue NE
Suite 101
Washington, DC 20017-4502

Canons 638 §§ 3, 4; 1293

Interpretation of Guidelines on Temporal Goods for Institutes of Consecrated Life and Societies of Apostolic Life

A professor contacted the Pontifical Council for Legislative Texts on the subject of temporal goods and the correct interpretation of particular guidelines for Economy at the Service of Charism and Mission, *a document produced by the Congregation for Institutes of Consecrated Life and Societies of Apostolic Life. What follows is the reply from the Pontifical Council for Legislative Texts and an unofficial English translation of the Council's letter.*

PONTIFICUM CONSILIUM DE LEGUM TEXTIBUS
Prot. N.
Città del Vaticano
03 dicembre 2018

Illustrissimo professore,

con la sua lettera del 12 novembre u.s., Ella ha chiesto il parere di questo Pontificio Consiglio riguardo due questioni legate alla corretta interpretazione del num. 81 e del num. 90 del documento della CIVCSVA "*Economia a servizio del carisma e della missione. Orientamenti*" alla luce del can. 638 § 3. Tali *Orientamenti*, in particolar modo nei numeri segnalati (n. 81 e n. 90) non intendono modificare la legge universale ma semplicemente <<richiamare ed esplicitare alcuni aspetti della normativa canonica sui beni temporali con particolare riferimento alla prassi della Congregazione per gli Instituti di vita consacrata e le Società di vita apostolica>> (*ivi*, n. 4).

Il n. 81 di tali orientamenti prevede che per tutte le alienazioni superiori all cifra massima stabilita dalla S. Sede a norma del can. 638 § 3 si richieda *ad validitatem* la licenza della CIVCSVA, indipendentemente dal fatto che tali beni appartengano o meno al patrimonio stabile dell'ente: quest'indicazione rispetta lo spirito dell'intero sistema dei controlli canonici sugli atti e sui beni degli IVC e delle SVA, pur nel rispetto del principio di sussidiarietà e della legittima autonomia degli istituti.

È prassi del Dicastero competente recepire per le singole Regioni la somma massima fissata dalle Conferenze Episcopali, pertanto se il valore del bene supera la somma massima fissata per le singole Regioni, a norma del can. 638 § 3, è necessario richiedere l'autorizzazione della Congregazione per gli Instituti di vita consacrata e le Società di vita apostolica, indpendentemente dal fatto che i beni siano ascritti o meno al patrimonio stabile, e questo perché la persona giuridica (Instituto di vita consacrata o Società di vita apostolica) può subire detrimento dall'alienazione di beni appartenenti non solo al patrimonio stabile (cfr. can. 638 §3).

Sembra suffragare tale interpretazione anche il *relator* del *Coetus Studii* <<*De Institutis Perfectionis*>>, che durante i lavori della *session XI* così afferma: <<Norma est sat simplex et facilis in praxis. In alienationibus ab Institutits faciendis, si summa non superset illam a Conferentia Episcoporum illius regionis determinatam, sufficit consensus moderatoris competentis ad normam iuris particularis. Si vero illam summam superset, semper recurrendum erit ad Apostolicam Sedem>> (in *Communicationes* XXVIII [1995], p. 120).

La richiesta dell'autorizzazione della Santa Sede deve essere presentata dal Superiore competente dell'Istituto a norma del diritto proprio; deve esprimere la giusta causa (can. 1293 § 1); deve definire le modalità in cui verrà impiegato il ricavato (can. 1294 § 2); deve essere allegata una documentazione peritale, possibilmente giurata (can. 1293 § 1, 2°); per i monasteri *sui iuris*, di cui nel can. 615, e per gli instituti di diritto diocesano, è necessario anche il consenso scritto dell'Ordinario del luogo (can. 638 § 4); il vescovo diocesano, circa i monasteri femminili affidati alla sua peculiar vigilanza, in deroga al can. 638 §4, dà, in quanto ordinario del luogo, il consenso scritto per particolari atti di amministrazione, se stabilito del diritto proprio (Istruzione *Cor Orans*, n. 81). Inoltre la CIVCSVA può richiedere, a norma del can. 1293 § 2, l'assunzione di altre cautele per evitare danni alla Chiesa.

Lo stesso sistema di controlli canonici è inoltre alla base del disposto del n. 90 degli *Orientamenti*, che, in caso di trasferimenti di beni ad enti civili, richiede *ad validitatem* la licenza della CIVCSVA quando il valore del bene da trasferire supera la somma massima stabilita, anche se la persona giuridica è legata all'istituto di vita consacrata o alla società di vita apostolica. Gli *Orientamenti*, circa gli *enti civili collegati all'Istituto*, affermano: <<Pur trattandosi di soggetti giuridicamente distinti, il collegamento di tali enti agli Instituti giustifica una particolare attenzione nella loro costituzione e nella loro gestione. L'attività di tali enti, infatti, può mettere a rischio la buona fama dell'Instituto e dar luogo, qualora

le leggi civili applicabili lo prevedano, a una responsabilità dell'Istituto per debiti dell'ente collegato. [...] In nessun caso il ricorso a enti civili, in qualunque forma realizzato, può essere utilizzato per eludere i controlli canonici>> (*Orientamenti*, n. 89). Inoltre, sembra chiaro che la persona giuridica civile , se è parimenti riconosciuta dall'autorità ecclesiastica secondo il can. 114 § 1 per mezzo di un decreto oppure in forza dello stesso diritto, è anche una persona giuridica nella Chiesa, in caso contrario è solo un ente civile. Sembrerebbe opportuno consigliare alle persone giuridiche civili *legate* alle persone giuridiche canoniche di mettere in atto, se del caso, gli opportuni procedimenti per un eventuale riconoscimento da parte dell'autorità ecclesiastica competente.

Con l'auspicio che tali rilievi possano risultare utili, profitto della circostanza per confermarmi, con sentimenti di cordiale ossequio,

dev.mo *in Domino*

+Filippo Iannone, O.C.
Presidente

+Juan Ignacio Arrieta
Segretario

UNOFFICIAL TRANSLATION

Pontifical Council for Legislative Texts
Prot. N.
Vatican City
December 3, 2018

Most illustrious Professor,

In your letter of last November 12 you requested the opinion of this Pontifical Council regarding two questions connected to the correct interpretation of number 81 and number 90 of the document from the CICLSAL *Economy at the service of charism and mission: Guidelines*, in light of canon 638 §3. These *Guidelines,* in particular those found in nn.81 and 90, do not modify the universal law but simply "recall and make explicit certain aspects of the canonical norms on temporal goods, with particular reference to the *praxis* of the Congregation for Institutes of Consecrated Life and Societies of Apostolic Life" (ibid, n.4).

Number 81 of these *Guidelines* foresees that in all alienations above the maximum amount established by the Holy See in accord with the norm of c. 638 §3, the permission of CICLSAL is required for validity. This is independent of whether or not such goods belong to the stable patrimony of the institute; this directive concerns the spirit of the entire system of canonical supervision over acts and goods of Institutes of Consecrated Life and Societies of Apostolic Life, while at the same time respecting the principle of subsidiarity and the legitimate autonomy of the institute.

It is the practice of the competent Dicastery to adopt for each region the maximum sum established by the Episcopal Conferences. Therefore, if the value of the goods exceeds the maximum sum established by the individual regions, according to the norm of canon 638 §3 it is necessary to request the authorization of the Congregation for the Institutes of Consecrated Life and Society of Apostolic Life, independently of whether the goods do or do not belong to the stable patrimony. This is because the juridic person (the Institute of Consecrated Life or Society of Apostolic Life), could suffer damage from the alienation of goods, not just those belonging to the stable patrimony (c. 638 §3)

The *relator* of the *Coetus Studii* "On Institutes of Perfection" also seems to support such an interpretation. During the work of Session XI he affirms, "The norm is simple enough and easy to put in practice. In alienations made by Institutes, if the sum does not exceed that which the Bishops' Conference in the region has determined, the consent of the competent moderator, according to particular law, suffices. If, however, it exceeds that sum, recourse must always be made to the Apostolic See" (in *Communicationes* XXVIII [1995], p. 120).

The request for the authorization of the Holy See should be presented by the competent Superior of the Institute according to the norm of its proper law. It should express a just cause (canon 1293 §1), and it should define the ways in which the revenue realized will be used (canon 1294 §1, 2°). For the monasteries *sui iuris* of canon 615 and for institutes of diocesan right the written consent of the local Ordinary is also necessary. In regard to monasteries of women entrusted to his particular vigilance, in derogation of canon 638 § 2, the diocesan bishop gives, as the local ordinary, his written consent for particular acts of administration if this is established by proper law (Instruction *Cor Orans*, n. 81, Additionally, the CICLSAL can request, according to the norm of canon 1293 §2, that other cautionary measures be taken to avoid harm to the Church.

The same system of canonical oversight is additionally the foundation of the dispositions of n. 90 of the *Guidelines*, namely, that in the case of transfer of a good to a civil entity, the permission of the CICLSAL is required for validity when the value of the goods to be transferred exceeds the maximum sum established, even if the juridic person is linked to the Institute of Consecrated Life or Society of Apostolic Life. With regard to the civil entities linked to the Institute, the *Guidelines* affirm: "Even though this deals with juridically distinct subjects, the bond of such entities to Institutes justifies a particular attention to their constitution and management. The activity of such entities, in fact, may place the good reputation of the Institute at risk and give rise, if the applicable civil laws provide for it, to a responsibility on the part of the Institute for the debts of the linked entity…In no case may recourse to civil entities, in whatever form it may be carried out, be used to evade canonical oversight." (*Guidelines,* n. 89) Furthermore, it seems clear that a civil juridic person, if it is equally recognized by ecclesiastical authority according to canon 114 §1 by means of a decree or by the law itself, is also a juridic person in the Church. In the case of the contrary, it is only a civil entity. It would seem opportune to advise civil juridic persons linked to canonical juridic persons to implement, if warranted, the appropriate procedures for a possible recognition on the part of competent ecclesiastical authority.

With the wish that such comments may prove useful, I take advantage of the circumstances to confirm myself, with sentiments of cordial esteem,

Your most devoted in the Lord,
+Filippo Iannone, O.C.
President

+Juan Ignacio Arrieta
Secretary

Canons 874 §2 and 877

Admission of Two Non-Catholic Witnesses to Baptism and Restrictions for Baptismal Register Annotations

A bishop sought the opinion of the Pontifical Council for Legislative Texts on a matter involving the admission of two non-Catholic witnesses to baptism, as well as appropriate parental annotations in the baptismal register for persons of the same sex and transgender persons. The Council's reply follows.

PONTIFICIUM CONSILIUM DE LEGUM TEXTIBUS
Prot. N.
Vatican City
15 November 2017

Your Excellency,

I write to respond to your letter of 28 June last, in which you asked for the opinion of this Pontifical Council regarding the admission of two non-Catholics as witnesses to baptism and the annotation of persons of the same sex and the so-called "transgender persons" as parents in the baptismal register.

After a careful consideration of the aforementioned matter, I am pleased to offer you the following indications.

Can. 874 §2 *CIC* establishes that a baptized non-Catholic may be admitted as witness to baptism only together with a Catholic sponsor. In this sense, our Pontifical Council considers that, given the particular role of the sponsor, two baptized non-Catholics may be admitted as witnesses to baptism only when there is a Catholic sponsor.

In the current Code, there is no specific law regarding the annotation of same sex couples or "transgender persons" as parents in the baptismal register. The term "parents" used by can. 877 *CIC* refers clearly to the father and the mother, man and woman created by God who are united in the sacrament of marriage (cf. can. 1055 §1 *CIC*) or to such a couple who adopted a child.

According to the disposition of can. 877 *CIC*, the parish priest must record in the baptismal register the name of the natural or adoptive father and mother (man and woman) or that of the unmarried mother (woman), as well as that of the father (man) if his paternity is proven by a public document.

The annotation of the same sex partners or "transgender persons" as parents would be contrary to the aforementioned canon and the teaching of Our Lord and of the Church on marriage as desired by God to be a union between a man and a woman. If one of the partners is the child's natural father or mother, he or she must be mentioned in the register; the other partner cannot be annotated.

Given the above indications, we do not consider it possible to annotate in the baptismal register two mothers or two fathers or a "transgender father" whose real nature is a woman or a "transgender mother" whose real nature is a man.

We hope that the above will be useful to you. Be assured of our own prayers and best fraternal wished in your ministry.

Sincerely yours in Christ,

+Francesco Card. Coccopalmerio
President

+Juan Ignacio Arrieta
Secretary

Canons 1676 §§1-2; 1678 §4; 1685 and 1687 §1

The Role of the Defender of the Bond

In the wake of the motu proprio Mitis Iudex Dominus Jesus (MIDI), *a priest wrote to the Pontifical Council for Legislative Texts about the role of the defender of the bond in marriage nullity procedure. In its reply, the Council addressed six questions and acknowledged the motivations for particular* MIDI *provisions. The reply follows.*

PONTIFICIUM CONSILIUM DE LEGUM TEXTIBUS
Prot. N.
Vatican City
24 January 2018

Reverend Father _________,

I refer to your letter to this Pontifical Council, in which you asked several questions regarding the role of the defender of the bond in the marriage nullity procedure in light of cann. 1676 §§1-2, 1685 and 1687 §1 of the motu proprio *Mitis Iudex Dominus Iesus* (MIDI), as well as regarding the transition from a juridical procedure to an administrative procedure *super rato* in the sense of can. 1678 §4 CIC/MIDI. The wording of the abovementioned canons is clear and does not need any authentic interpretation. Your questions concern instead the correct application of the norm.

As to your first five questions, the following can be noted. Can. 1676 §1 CIC/MIDI clearly requires the judicial vicar to order that a copy of the *libellus*, once admitted, be communicated to the defender of the bond. The latter should then give his observations within fifteen days. Can. 1676 §2 CIC/MIDI holds that the judicial vicar can only fix the formula of the doubt once he has received the observations by the defender of the bond or once the term of fifteen days mentioned in §1 has expired.

Can. 1685 CIC/MIDI states that "the judicial vicar, by the same decree which determines the formula of the doubt, having names an instructor and an assessor, cites all who must take part to a session (omnes … qui in ea interesse debent), which in turn must be held within thirty days according to can. 1686." This undoubtedly includes the defender of the bond. If it turns out to be impossible to conclude the instruction of the case in one session, the defender of the bond must also be cited for all successive sessions.

Finally, can. 1687 §1 CIC/MIDI specifies that, regarding the briefer process, the diocesan bishop has to consider the observations of the defender of the bond (*perpensis animadversionibus defensoris vinculi*) before rendering his sentence. Of course, the diocesan bishop is not bound to follow the reasoning proposed by the defender of the bond but his reasoning could nevertheless indicate to the Bishop whether the case has to be further investigated by the ordinary process (cf. can. 1687 §1).

All these provisions are motivated by the desire to protect the contentious nature of the judicial procedure, as well as the right of defense. It is outside the competence of our Pontifical Council to determine whether the partial non-respect of these canons in a particular case amounts to an irremediable nullity in the sense of can. 1620, 7° CIC.

Your final question concerns the application of can. 1678 §4 CIC/MIDI. It results from the canon, as well as from an earlier Circular Letter by the Congregation for the Sacraments dated 20 December 1986 (Art. 7), that there is no dogmatic or any normative obstacle to a transition from a judicial nullity procedure to an administrative procedure *super rato*, if there is a very probable doubt (*dubium valde probabile*) as to whether the marriage was ever consummated. Whereas the said Circular Letter still requires the consent of both parties (*accedente consensus utriusque*), can. 1678 §4 CIC/MIDI only requires that the parties be heard (*auditis partibus*), even though it might still be prudent to evaluate the parties' opinion. It clearly follows, however, from the use of the term '*potest*', that the college of judges or the single judge is not obliged to suspend the judicial process. It is left to the discretion of the judge(s) to decide upon the expediency of such a transition to the administrative process *super rato*. Finally, it should be noted that prior to the granting of the dispensation *super rato*, the judicial process is only suspended, not terminated.

In the hope to have given you some helpful information, we assure you of our best and prayerful wished for your ministry.

Sincerely yours *in Domino*,

+ Juan Ignacio Arrieta Segretario	Mons. Markus Graulich SDB Sotto-Segretario

Canon 1680 §2

Clarifications on *Mitis Iudex Dominus Iesus* Provisions

A priest contacted the Pontifical Council for Legislative Texts, seeking clarification on the expression of canon 1680 §2 *in the motu proprio* Mitis Iudex Dominus Iesus, *as well as guidance on the provisions that determine the appeal process. The Council's reply follows.*

PONTIFICIUM CONSILIUM DE LEGUM TEXTIBUS
Prot. N.
Vatican City
February 20, 2017

Dear Father ___________,

I write in response to your letter of 7 November last, in which you posed three questions to this Pontifical Council regarding the m. p. *Mitis Iudex Dominus Iesus* (*MIDI*). Having examined your inquiries, in collaboration with some of our consultors, I am pleased to offer the following indications.

Concerning your first question, this Dicastery holds that the expression of can. 1680 §2 in the m.p. "*MIDI*" <<*si appellation mere dilatoria evidenter appareat, tribunal collegiale, suo decreto, sententiam prioris instantiae* ***confirmet***>>, taken in the context of the entire can. 1680, must be understood in the sense that the collegiate tribunal of second instance, having reached moral certainty after the examination of the acts and the judgment of first instance as well as the appeals and the observations of the Defender of the Bond, and having verified that the appeal has manifestly dilatory purposes *evidenter appareat*, must confirm by decree the judgment of the first instance.

Regarding your second question about the possibility of appeal to the Metropolitan Tribunal by dioceses that are part of the Inter-diocesan Tribunal whose suppression was sought, we maintain that, so long as the Inter-diocesan Tribunal of Appeal is not suppressed and the link with which it was formally established is not legitimately changed, the aforementioned dioceses cannot appeal to the Metropolitan Tribunal.

With respect to your third question, we consider that the *acta* of the *Processus brevior* are included in the same restrictive regime that the law provides for judicial acts of matrimonial processes.

I hope that the above information will be helpful to you. Be assured of my best prayerful wishes for your ministry.

Sincerely yours *in Domino,*

+ Francesco Card. Coccopalmerio
President

+ Juan Ignacio Arrieta
Secretary

Other Vatican Documents

Apostolic Letter Issued Motu Proprio
By the Supreme Pontiff Francis
Communis Vita

WHICH PROVIDES FOR THE MODIFICATION OF SEVERAL NORMS OF THE CODE OF CANON LAW

Life in community is an essential element of religious life, and "religious are to live in their own religious house and are not to be absent from it except with the permission of their superior" (Can. 665 §1 CIC). The experience of recent years has, however, demonstrated that situations occur that are related to illegitimate absences from the religious house, during which religious distance themselves from the jurisdiction of the legitimate Superior and at times cannot be located.

The Code of Canon Law requires the Superior to seek out the illegitimately absent religious in order to help him or her to return and persevere in his or her vocation (cf. can. 665 §2 CIC). Quite often, however, it may happen that the Superior is unable to locate the absent religious. Pursuant to the Code of Canon Law, after at least six months of illegitimate absence (cf. can. 696 CIC), it is possible to begin the process of dismissal by the institute, according to the established procedure (cf. can. 697 CIC). However, when the religious' place of residence is unknown, it becomes difficult to accord juridical certainty to the *de facto* situation.

Therefore, notwithstanding what is established by the law on dismissal following six months of illegitimate absence, in order to help institutes apply the necessary discipline and be able to proceed to the dismissal of the illegitimately absent religious, especially in cases in which his or her location is unknown, I have decided to add to can. 694 §1 CIC, among the reasons for dismissal *ipso facto* from the institute, also a prolonged illegitimate absence from the religious house lasting at least 12 consecutive months, with the same procedure described in can. 694 §2 CIC. In order to produce juridical effects, the statement of the case by the Major Superior must be confirmed by the Holy See; for institutes of diocesan right, the confirmation rests with the Bishop of the principal See.

The introduction of this new article to §1 of can. 694 requires, moreover, a modification of can. 729 with regard to secular institutes, for which the application of discretionary dismissal for illegitimate absence is not provided.

Considering the foregoing, I now dispose as follows:

Art. 1. Can. 694 CIC is entirely replaced by the following text:

§1. A religious must be held as dismissed *ipso facto* from an institute who:

1. has defected notoriously from the Catholic faith;
2. has contracted marriage or attempted it, even only civilly;
3. has been illegitimately absent from the religious house, pursuant to can. 665 §2, for 12 consecutive months, taking into account that the location of the religious himself or herself may be unknown.

§2. In such cases the Major Superior, with his or her Council and without hesitation, having gathered the evidence, must issue the statement of the case so that the dismissal may be juridically constituted.

§3. In the case envisaged by §1 n. 3, in order to be juridically constituted, this statement must be confirmed by the Holy See; for institutes of diocesan right the confirmation rests with the Bishop of the principal See.

Art. 2. Can. 729 CIC is entirely replaced by the following text:

Dismissal of a member of the institute proceeds pursuant to cann. 694 §1, 1 and 2; and 695. The constitutions may also define other causes for dismissal, provided that they be commensurately serious, external, attributable and juridically proven, and that the procedure established in cann. 697-700 also be observed. The provisions of can. 701 are applicable to the dismissed member.

As deliberated with this Apostolic Letter issued Motu Proprio, I dispose that it take firm and permanent effect, despite any matters to the contrary even if worthy of special mention, and that it be promulgated by publication in *L'Osservatore Romano*, entering into force on 10 April 2019, and thereafter be published in the official commentary *Acta Apostolicae Sedis.*[1]

Given in Rome at Saint Peter's
on 19 March 2019, Solemnity of Saint Joseph
Seventh Year of My Pontificate

FRANCIS

1 English translation from *L'Osservatore Romano*, Friday, March 29, 2019.

Motu Proprio Regarding Pontifical Commission *Ecclesia Dei*

With a Letter issued Motu Proprio on 17 January, the Pope has decommissioned the Pontifical Commission 'Ecclesia Dei' – instituted in 1988 in order to facilitate "the full ecclesial communion of priests, seminarians, communities or individual men and women religious connected with the Fraternity founded by Archbishop Marcel Lefebvre " – transferring its tasks "entirely" to the Congregation for the Doctrine of Faith. The following is a translation of the Letter in L'osservatore Romano.

Apostolic Letter issued MOTU PROPRIO
regarding the Pontifical Commission
Ecclesia Dei

For over 30 years the Pontifical Commission *Ecclesia Dei*, instituted with the Motu Proprio *Ecclesia Dei Adflicta* of 2 July 1988, has carried out with sincere solicitude and praiseworthy concern the task of collaborating with the Bishops and the Dicasteries of the Roman Curia, in facilitating the full ecclesial communion of priests, seminarians, communities or individual men and women religious connected with the Fraternity founded by Archbishop Marcel Lefebvre, who wished to remain united to the Successor of Peter in the Catholic Church, preserving their own spiritual and liturgical traditions.[1]

In this way, it was able to exercise its own authority and competence in the name of the Holy See over these societies and associations, until otherwise provided.[2]

Subsequently, by virtue of the Motu Proprio *Summorum Pontificum* of 7 July 2007, the Pontifical Commission extended the authority of the Holy See to those Institutes and Religious Communities which had adhered to the extraordinary form of the Roman Rite and had assumed the precedent traditions of religious life, supervising the observance and application of the provisions established.[3]

---

1 Cf. Ioannes Paulus PP. II, Litterae Apostolicae 'Motu proprio datae', *Ecclesia Dei adflicta*, 2 Iulii 1988 ,*AAS*, LXXX (1988), 12 (15 Nov. 1988), 1495-1498, 6a.

2 Cf. *Rescriptum ex Audientia Sanctissimi*, 18 Oct. 1988, *AAS*, LXXXII (1990), 5 (3 Maii 1990), 533-534, 6.

3 Cf. Benedictus PP. XVI, Litterae Apostolicae 'Motu proprio datae', *Summorum Pontificum*, 7 Iulii 2007, *AAS*, XCIX (2007), 9 (7 Sept. 2007), 777-781, 12.

Two years later, my Venerable Predecessor Benedict XVI, with the Motu Proprio *Ecclesiae Unitatem* of 2 July 2009, reorganized the structure of the Pontifical Commission, in order to make it more suited to the new situation created by the remission of the excommunication of the four Bishops consecrated without pontifical mandate. And, furthermore, considering that after this act of grace, the questions addressed by the same Pontifical Commission were of a primarily doctrinal nature, he connected it more systematically to the Congregation for the Doctrine of the Faith, while maintaining its initial aims, but modifying its structure.[4]

Now, as the *Feria* IV of the Congregation for the Doctrine of the Faith of 15 November 2017 formulated the request that dialogue between the Holy See and the Priestly Fraternity of Saint Pius X be conducted directly by the aforementioned Congregation, as the matters being addressed are of a doctrinal nature, to which request I gave my approval *in Audientia* with the Prefect on 24 November 2017 and this proposal was accepted by the Plenary Session of the same Congregation celebrated from 23 to 26 January 2018, after ample reflection, I have arrived at the following decision.

Considering that today the conditions which led the holy Pontiff John Paul II to institute the Pontifical Commission *Ecclesia Dei* have changed;

noting that the Institutes and Religious Communities which customarily celebrate in the extraordinary form have today found proper stability of number and of life;

recognizing that the aims and questions addressed by the Pontifical Commission *Ecclesia Dei* are of a predominantly doctrinal order;

and wishing that these aims be made ever more evident to the conscience of the ecclesial communities,

with this Apostolic Letter 'Motu Proprio data',

I decree that

1. The Pontifical Commission *Ecclesia Dei*, instituted on 2 July 1988 with the Motu Proprio *Ecclesia Dei Adflicta*, is decommmissioned.

2. The tasks of the Commission in question are assigned entirely to the Congregation for the Doctrine of the Faith, within which will be established a special Section committed to continue the work of

4 Cf. Benedictus PP. XVI, Litterae Apostolicae 'Motu proprio datae', *Ecclesiae unitatem*, 2 Iulii 2009, *AAS*, CI (2009), 8 (7 Aug. 2009), 710-711, 5.

supervision, promotion and protection conducted thus far by the decommissioned Pontifical Commission *Ecclesia Dei*.

3. The financial report of the Pontifical Commission returns to the ordinary accounting of the aforementioned Congregation.

Furthermore, I establish that this Motu Proprio — to be observed notwithstanding anything to the contrary, even if worthy of specific mention — be promulgated by publication in the 19 January 2019 issue of *L'Osservatore Romano*, entering immediately into force, and that it be inserted thereafter into the official register of the Holy See, the *Acta Apostolicae Sedis*.

Given in Rome, at Saint Peter's
on 17 January 2019
Sixth Year of My Pontificate

FRANCIS

Address of His Holiness Pope Francis to the Officials of the Tribunal of the Roman Rota For the Inauguration of the Judicial Year

* * *

Clementine Hall
Tuesday, 29 January 2019

Excellency,

Dear prelate auditors,

I address to you my warm greeting, beginning with the dean, whom I thank for his words. I greet those taking part in this meeting: the officials, the lawyers and the other collaborators of the Apostolic Tribunal of the Roman Rota. To all of you I offer my sincere good wishes for the legal year we inaugurate today.

The society in which we live is increasingly secularized, and does not favour the growth of faith, with the consequence that Catholic faithful struggle to bear witness to a style of life in accordance with the Gospel, also with regard to the Sacrament of marriage. In such a context, it is necessary for the Church, in all her articulations, to act in harmony to offer adequate spiritual and pastoral support. In the daily ministry in the service of Christian marriage, you have the experience of two fundamental cornerstones, not only of theology and canon law of marriage, but also and first of all of the very essence of Christ's Church: *unity* and *fidelity*. These two matrimonial assets, indeed, before being, or rather *in order to be* legal obligations of any conjugal union in Christ, must be the epiphany of baptismal faith.

So as to be validly contracted, marriage requires of each of the betrothed a full *unity* and harmony with the other, so that, through the mutual exchange of their respective human, moral and spiritual riches – almost by way of communicating vessels – the two spouses become a single entity. Marriage also requires the commitment of fidelity, which absorbs all of life, becoming a stable *consortium totius vitae* (canon 1135).

Unity and fidelity are two important and necessary values not only among spouses, but in general in interpersonal and social relations. We are all aware of the inconveniences that are caused, in civil coexistence, by unfulfilled promises, the lack of fidelity to the word given and to commitments undertaken.

Unity and *fidelity*. These two assets, indispensable and constitutive of marriage, must not only be adequately illustrated to future spouses, but also demand the pastoral action of the Church, especially of bishops and priests, to accompany the family in the different phases of its formation and of its development. Such pastoral action naturally cannot be limited to the completion of paperwork, while this may be necessary and is to be carried out with care. There is a need for a triple preparation for marriage: remote, near and permanent. It is advisable for this latter to include in a serious and structural way the various phases of married life, through an accurate formation, intended to nurture in spouses the awareness of the values and commitments proper to their vocation.

The main subjects of this matrimonial formation, by virtue of their office and ministry, are pastors; however, it is more opportune than ever before – indeed, necessary – to involve the ecclesial communities in their various components, who are co-responsible in this pastoral care under the guidance of the diocesan bishop or the parish priest. The duty is therefore *in solidum*, with the primary responsibility of pastors and the active participation of the community in promoting marriage and in accompanying families with spiritual and formative support.

To understand this pastoral need, it will be good for us to consider, in the Scriptures, the experience of the holy spouses Aquila and Priscilla. They were among the most faithful companions of the mission of Saint Paul, who called them with grateful affection his *sinergoi*, that is his full collaborators in the concerns and the work of the Apostle. This high recognition on the part of Paul for the missionary work of these spouses is striking and moving; and at the same time it can be acknowledged how this synergy was a precious gift of the Spirit to the first Christian communities. Let us ask, therefore, that today too the Spirit give to the Church priests capable of appreciating and valuing the charisms of spouses with robust faith and apostolic spirit, such as Aquila and Priscilla.

The constant and permanent pastoral care of the Church for the good of marriage and of the family demands to be realized through various pastoral means: approaching the Word of God, especially through the *lectio divina*; spiritual discussion and direction; the participation in family groups and charitable service, to develop exchange with other families and openness to the needs of the most disadvantaged.

On the other hand, spouses who live their marriage with *generous unity* and with *faithful love*, supporting each other with the grace of the Lord and with the necessary support of the ecclesial community, represent in turn a precious pastoral help to the Church. Indeed, they offer to all an example of true love and become witnesses and co-workers in the fruitfulness of the Church herself. Truly many Christian couples are a silent prayer for all, a "weekday" prayer, I would say, for every day, and we must unfortunately note that a couple that lives for many years together does not make the news – this is sad – while scandals, separations and divorces do (cf. *Homily at Santa Marta*, Friday 18 May 2018).

This is the good news: that fidelity is possible, because it is a gift, in spouses as in priests. This is the news that should render stronger and comforting even the ministry of bishops and priests, faithful and full of love; just as the love and conjugal faithfulness of the spouses Aquila and Priscilla were of comfort to Paul and Apollo.

Dear prelate auditors, I reiterate to each one of you my gratitude for the good you do for the people of God, serving justice through your verdicts. Besides the importance of the judgement itself for the interested parties, they contribute to the correct interpretation of matrimonial law. This law is places at the service of the *salus animarum* and of the faith of spouses. Therefore, we understand the punctual reference to the verdicts of the Rota to the principles of Catholic doctrine, with regard to the natural idea of marriage, with its related duties and rights, and even more so concerning its sacramental reality.

Thank you very much for your work! I invoke divine assistance upon it, and I heartily impart my Apostolic Blessing. And please, do not forget to pray for me. Thank you!

ADVISORY OPINIONS

Introductory Note

The following opinions were assembled by the members of the Publications Advisory Board from among those submitted to the Society for publication. The opinions carry only the weight of the persons named at the end of each opinion. They do not represent the opinion of the diocese or institution to which the author is affiliated, nor that of the Canon Law Society of America. Advisory opinions are not authentic interpretations of the law, but reflect the scholarly and practical insights of the contributors.

The opinions are arranged according to the canons of the *Code of Canon Law* and the *Code of Canons of the Eastern Churches*. The original questions have been abbreviated or summarized, and the opinions lightly edited to protect the anonymity of the inquirer and to conform to the style of Canon Law Society of America publications.

The Publications Advisory Board expresses gratitude to the canonists who participated in this year's publication. The continued success of this annual project is a result of their willingness to share their time and talent in service to this important work.

The Canon Law Society of America is interested in receiving opinions that members have formulated in response to specific inquiries, and inquiries in need of responses. It also welcomes the participation of members who wish to be involved in this annual project by offering to render opinions to inquiries received by the Board.

Inquiries or contributions may be directed to:

Canon Law Society of America
415 Michigan Avenue NE
Suite 101
Washington, DC 20017-4502

INTRODUCTORY NOTE

Canons 125; 205; 219; 573-606; 641-661; 675

Suitability of Persons with Transsexualism

A superior asked: What aspects of the elements of suitability prescribed by law for admission to vows in consecrated life are to be examined regarding persons with transsexualism?

Opinion

Nature of Consecrated Life

Oxford dictionaries define suitability as the quality of being right or appropriate for a particular person, purpose, or situation. Examining suitability for consecrated life, therefore, must begin with the nature of religious life. Suitability includes, freedom of consent, ability to function as a public person in the name of the Church, and capacity to live the life of the institute.

The ecclesial nature of consecrated life is defined in canon law (cc. 573-606),[1] which discusses the norms common to all forms of life consecrated by the evangelical counsels. O'Hara states,

> Canon 573 is a combination of both theological and juridical elements. Following the wording of the canon, the choice of consecrated life is an explication of the prior choice for Christ in baptism. Both theologically and juridically, the choice for consecrated life is to be a total dedication of the person, in a spirit-filled life delineated specifically to the honor of God, the upbuilding of the Church, and the salvation of the world."[2]

The particular living out of the evangelical counsels is embodied in the heritage and law of the particular institute. An institute came into being by the canonical erection by the competent Church authority and remains bound to ecclesial governance.

Those who have the competence to admit candidates to the novitiate, have the responsibility to consider the health, suitable character and sufficient maturity

1 Code of Canon Law Latin-English Edition, New English Translation, Canon Law Society of America, Washington, DC 20064. All canons where quoted are taken from this edition. The *Code of Canons of Eastern Churches* on the topic are Canons 410-572.

2 Ellen O'Hara, C.S.J., *A Handbook on Canons 573-746*, The Liturgical Press, Collegeville, Minnesota, 1985, p. 32.

of an applicant. (C. 642). These areas are to be examined as well as the qualities required by universal and proper law for life in a particular institute. The use of experts to attest to the ability of the applicant to live the life can be used if necessary. Andrés states, "This is a matter of personal qualities that must be had by the candidate, not a matter of impediments, proofs, or reports."[3] Canons 641–661 govern the admission of candidates and the formation of members. Only those judged suitable are to be admitted.

The first quality mentioned in C. 642 is health.

> The health of the candidate must be understood in its biological and psychic dimensions, keeping in mind the unity of the person. It is not so much the lack of illness, but the subjective state of the entire well-being in general of the person, in its physical, spiritual, psychic, social, and familial dimensions.[4]

Suitable character and sufficient maturity may be assessed in behavioral indicators. This is subjective judgment and relies on the well-founded practices of the institute and the mature experience of formation personnel.

In the Encyclical Letter *Veritas Splendor*, John Paul II stated, "the Magisterium has the duty to state that some trends of theological thinking and certain philosophical affirmations are incompatible with revealed truth."[5] In addition, the *Catechism of the Catholic Church* states, "It is this Magisterium's task to preserve God's people from deviations and defections and to guarantee them the objective possibility of professing the true faith without error."[6]

The nature of human sexuality is articulated in the *Catechism of the Catholic Church* No. 2333[7]. It states,

> Everyone, man and woman, should acknowledge and accept his sexual identity. Physical, moral, and spiritual difference and complementarity are oriented toward the good of marriage and the flourishing of family life. The harmony of the couple and society depends in part on the way in which the complementarity, needs and mutual support between the sexes are lived out.

---

3 Domingo J. Andrés, cmf, Exegetical Commentary on the Code of Canon Law, Wilson & Lafleur Montreal, Canada, Midwest Theological Forum Chicago, Illinois, 2004, p. 1695.

4 Ibid., p. 1696.

5 John Paul II Encyclical *Veritas Splendor*, 6 August 1993, number 29.

6 Catechism of the Catholic Church, Second Edition, *Libreria Editrice Vaticana*, First Printing, March 2000, Eighteenth Printing, December 2007, p. 235.

7 Ibid., p. 560.

Veritas Splendor paragraph 48 states, "since the human person cannot be reduced to a freedom which is self-designing, but entails a particular spiritual and bodily structure, the primordial moral requirement of loving and respecting the person as an end and never as a mere means also implies, by its very nature, respect for certain fundamental goods, without which one would fall into relativism and arbitrariness."

In the Encyclical Letter *Laudato Sí* (2015), Pope Francis states,

> Learning to accept our body, to care for it and to respect its fullest meaning, is an essential element of any genuine human ecology. Also, valuing one's own body in its femininity or masculinity is necessary if I am going to be able to recognize myself in an encounter with someone who is different. In this way we can joyfully accept the specific gifts of another man or woman, the work of God the Creator, and find mutual enrichment. It is not a healthy attitude which would seek to cancel out sexual difference because it no longer knows how to confront it.[8]

In the Apostolic Exhortation *Amoris Laetitia* (2016), Pope Francis states,

> It needs to be emphasized that 'biological sex and the socio-cultural role of sex (gender) can be distinguished but not separated.' …It is one thing to be understanding of human weakness and the complexities of life, and another to accept ideologies that attempt to sunder what are inseparable aspects of reality.[9]

The Congregation for Institutes of Consecrated Life and Societies of Apostolic Life published *Directives on Formation in Religious Formation* (1990). The document is given the weight of an Instruction according to canon 34 of the *Code of Canon Law*. In the section "Sexuality and Formation," the document states,

> Moreover, men and women must become aware of their specific place in the plan of God, of the unique contribution which respectively they should make to the work of salvation. Future religious should thus be offered the possibility of reflecting on the role of sexuality in the divine plan of creation and salvation. In this context reasons must be given and understood to explain why those who do not seem to be able to overcome their homosexual tendencies, or who maintain that is is

8 Pope Francis Encyclical *Laudato Sí*, 2015, number 155.
9 Pope Francis Apostolic Exhortation *Amoris Laetitia* 2016, number 56.

> possible to adopt a third way, 'living in an ambiguous state between celibacy and marriage' must be dismissed from the religious life.[10]

Helpful to the discussion is the "Brief Statement on Transgenderism"[11] from the National Catholic Bioethics Center. It states,

> The notion of being able to change one's sex, most radically through surgical intervention, has increasingly become a part of public awareness and social discourse. The boldness of the gender ideology movement has now brought it to the forefront.

And,

> Gender transitioning insists on affirming a false identity and in many cases, mutilation of the body in support of that falsehood.

And further,

> the concept of gender transitioning, however, stands in radical opposition to a proper understanding of the nature of the human person. It presupposes that there is a 'self' that is separate from the body, which happens to find itself in a body and which might therefore be in the wrong body. Yet the human person is a full body-soul unity, not a 'ghost in the machine' or a spirit inhabiting the body. A particular person does not merely have a body: he or she is that body. In the words of Pope St. John Paul II, the 'human body expresses the person.'

Similar content can be found at the Notre Dame Center for Ethics and Culture.[12]

There exist persons whose disconnect between their self-perception of sexual identity and the physical reality causes them a sense of great discomfort. Pastoral sensitivity and care for the welfare of the person must accompany the assessment of the person not suitable for religious life.

---

10 Congregation for Institutes of Consecrated Life and Societies of Apostolic Life: Directives on Formation in Religious Institutes (1990), number 39-41.

11 Brief Statement on Transgenderism, the National Catholic Bioethics Center, February 22, 2017. See this statement for statements on human anthropology and gender, and on ethical implications in Catholic health care and Catholic educational institutions.

12 The Notre Dame Center for Ethics and Culture, https://ethicscenter.nd.edu.

Suitability prescribed by law

Canon 219 states all Christ's faithful have the right to immunity from any kind of coercion in choosing a state in life. Referring to this right, Navarrete[13] makes the following observation.

> This right, nevertheless, by no means implies a right to embrace any state of Christian life whatsoever. For plainly each and every state requires, besides natural ability and juridical capacity, the suitability prescribed by law, the existence of which in individual cases (if it is a question of consecrated life) is determined by the authorities competent to admit candidates.[14]

Canon 675 states in institutes dedicated to works of the apostolate, apostolic action pertains to their very nature. Paragraph §3 states "apostolic action, to be exercised in the name and by the mandate of the Church, is to be carried out in the communion of the Church." Communion with the Church is defined in Canon 205 as being "joined with Christ in its visible structure by the bonds of profession of faith, the sacraments, and ecclesiastical governance." Being united with the Church in this way includes the teachings of the Magisterium, Christian anthropology, sacred apologetics and sacred tradition.

Examining the suitability of a candidate must include the recognition that he or she is able to assume ministry in the name of the Church. Overt conflict with this premise constitutes sufficient reason to deny entrance into the novitiate or admission to vows.

Admission to vows in consecrated life

Canons 641-661 govern the admission of candidates and the formation of members. Canon 643 §1, 4° states that one is invalidly admitted to the novitiate "who enters the institute induced by force, grave fear, or malice, or the one whom a superior, induced in the same way, has received." Hite states,

> Each of the prohibited influences has its particular effect on the freedom of consent of either the candidate or the admitting superior, which like any other juridic act in the Church must be freely made C.125. Force

13 Urbano Cardinal Navarrete, SJ, "Transsexualism and the Canonical Order," National Catholic Bioethics Quarterly 14.1 (Spring 2014):105-118. This is the first authorized English translation made by Michael Miller, MA. It originally appeared as *"Transexualismus et ordo canonicus," Periodica de re canonica* 86.1 (1997): 101-124. It provides a readable description of typology of transsexuality. Citation at p. 117.

14 Ibid., p. 117.

> and grave fear or fraud depending on its effect on the will may destroy or diminish consent. In either case it invalidates it.[15]

Among the behavioral characteristics of the person with transsexualism often demonstrated are self-preoccupation, self-perception not aligned with physical reality, self-referenciality, symptoms of gender dysphoria, and demands to be accepted or treated as the preferred gender or sex. These characteristics are evidence the person is unprepared to undertake the life of the institute. Such characteristics place a grave burden on common life and on the credibility of the person to function as a public minister of the Church.

Persons with transexxualism

Navarrete states,

> no one can fail to see that true transsexuals are not suited to consecrated life because in the first place they lack the degree of psychological equilibrium that is required in order to lead that kind of life. But there is a deeper reason why a transsexual is not suited to and perhaps not capable of consecrated life: namely, the disconnect that the transsexual suffers between his psychological perception of his own sex and his phenotypic sex makes it impossible to dedicate himself within the special structure of consecrated life either in a male institute or in a female institute.[16]

If manifest prior to admission to the novitiate, the person with transsexualism is not to be admitted. If manifested during the probation period, the candidate cannot be admitted to vows.

One not approved for final profession is to depart the institute. Equity and evangelical charity are to be observed.

Therese Guerin Sullivan, SP, JCL

15 Jordan Hite, T.O.R. A Handbook on Canons 573-746, the Liturgical Press, Collegeville, Minnesota, 1985, p. 123.

16 Urbano Cardinal Navarrete, SJ, "*Transsexualism and the Canonical Order*", National Catholic Bioethics Quarterly 14.1 (Spring 2014): p. 117.

Canons 573 and 579

Bishop Seeks Permission

I am the bishop of a diocese. Over twenty years ago a community of sisters was erected as a Public Association of the Faithful. They are stable and their membership has increased. They have excellent financial resources. Their apostolate is meeting the needs of the people. They would like to be established as a religious institute of diocesan right. I am in agreement with them. Over the years I have had conversations with officials from several dicasteries in Rome. They have been very supportive. Is this enough to satisfy the need to consult with Rome before I go forward with the decree of erection?

Opinion

In order to respond to your question, it might be helpful to start by giving a brief overview of two important canons. Canon 573[1] is the cornerstone for religious and secular institutes because it is both theological and juridical. Its first paragraph clearly indicates that consecrated life is a total dedication of an individual. Through the profession of the evangelical counsels, the Spirit-filled life of this person honors God as well as contributing to the upbuilding of the Church and the salvation of the world. This is a new and special consecration that more fully expresses the commitment every Christian makes at baptism.[2] The second paragraph adds the juridic elements. It indicates that consecrated life is lived in an institute canonically erected by the competent authority of the Church. It then states that through vows or other sacred bonds according to the proper law of the institute, the person professes the evangelical counsels of chastity, poverty and obedience. The choice to profess them is a free one.

1 *Codex Iuris Canonici auctoritate Ioannis Pauli PP. II promulgatus* (Vatican City: Libreria Editrice Vaticana, 1983). English translation: *Code of Canon Law, Latin-English Edition: New English Translation* (Washington, DC: Canon Law Society of America, 2012). Canon 731 is the relevant canon for Societies of Apostolic Life.

2 Second Vatican Council, dogmatic constitution *Lumen gentium*, 42-44, November 21, 1964: *AAS* 57 (1965) 5–71. English translation: http://www.vatican.va/archive/hist_councils/ii_vatican_council/documents/vat-ii_const_19641121_lumen-gentium_en.html, accessed February 2019; Second Vatican Council, decree *Perfectae caritatis*, 1. October 28, 1965: *AAS* 58 (1966) 702–712. English translation: http://www.vatican.va/archive/hist_councils/ii_vatican_council/documents/vat-ii_decree_19651028_perfectae-caritatis_en.html, accessed February 2019.

The competence of the diocesan bishop to canonically erect an institute in his territory is stated in canon 579.[3] It is conditioned on the requirement of a prior consultation with the Apostolic See. Why? Vatican II spoke to this issue by stating that when it is proposed to establish a new religious institute serious questions must be asked. They include looking at whether this new institute is necessary or useful and whether it will be able to increase its membership. When these questions are not pondered carefully, it may be imprudent to erect a new institute.[4] Post-conciliar documents such as *Mutuae relationes*[5] and *Vita Consecrata*[6] also speak to the care that must be taken. Since the act of erection of an institute by the diocesan bishop is a gift to the entire Church, the act has implications that go far beyond the diocese. Therefore, it is important that the Holy See be consulted because her experience can help the bishop make a judgement about this matter. If the bishop receives the *nihil obstat,* it becomes a strong supportive confirmation of his own understanding.

In order to evaluate the situation and, hopefully, receive the *nihil obstat* the diocesan bishop needs to send the following items to the *Congregation for Institutes of Consecrated Life and Societies of Apostolic Life*: (1) the name(s) of the founder or foundress and the first superior general along with a *curriculum vitae* of each, (2) an historical-juridical account of the association from its beginnings, including the decree of erection as a public association of the faithful, (3) the constitution and the directory of the institute revised in accordance with the Code of Canon Law, (4) where applicable, a picture of the religious dress of both a professed member and a novice, (5) up-to-date statistics of the membership, including the year of birth and of temporary and perpetual profession,[7] the place and diocese where houses are located, and the works of the institute,[8] (6) an account of the financial patrimony of the institute including debts, (7) statements regarding any extraordinary experiences or particular devotions and whether in

3 Canon 732 applies canon 579 to Societies of Apostolic Life.

4 *Perfectae caritatis*, 19.

5 Congregations for Religious and Secular Institutes and for Bishops, norms *Mutuae relationes*, May 14, 1978: *AAS* 70 (1978) 473–506, paragraph 51. English translation: http://www.vatican.va/roman_curia/congregations/ccscrlife/documents/rc_con_ccscrlife_doc_14051978_mutuae-relationes_en.html, accessed February 2019.

6 John Paul II, post-synodal apostolic exhortation *Vita consecrata*, March 25, 1996: *AAS* 88 (1996) 377–487, paragraph 36. English translation: http://w2.vatican.va/content/john-paul-ii/en/apost_exhortations/documents/hf_jp-ii_exh_25031996_vita-consecrata.html, accessed February 2019.

7 For erection as an institute of diocesan right, the required number is about 40 members who have professed perpetual private vows. For erection as an institute of pontifical right, the number is about 100. For a monastery of canon 615, the number is different. Number 39 of *Cor orans*, the instruction on women's contemplative life, indicates that there must be 8 nuns in solemn vows.

8 For secular institutes there is no listing of houses as there is for religious institutes since there is no obligation to common life or corporate works.

the diocese of origin there already exists another institute with the same purpose and name, (8) testimonial letters from the diocesan bishops of those diocese in which the institute is represented, and (9) the "deposit" of 500 euros.[9]

The aforementioned testimonial letters are to be sent directly to the Holy See giving the opinion of the bishops about the following matters: usefulness, stability, discipline of the institute, formation of members, government, administration of goods, liturgical and sacramental dimensions, and a sense of being with the Church, particularly in regard to the observances of ecclesiastical discipline as expressed in the law of the Church and in the diocesan directives. Once the *nihil obstat* is given, the diocesan bishop approves the constitution and erects the group as an institute of diocesan right through a formal decree.

Is the *nihil obstat* required for validity? A rescript on canon 579 on the establishment of diocesan institutes issued on May 11, 2016 responds in the affirmative to this question. It says,

> The Congregation for Institutes of Consecrated Life and Societies of Apostolic Life, aware that every new Institute of consecrated life even when it comes into being and develops within a Particular Church is a gift for the whole Church, and acknowledging the need to prevent new Institutes from being established on the diocesan level that lack the proper discernment and to ascertain the true origin of each charism that would define the specific features that would receive consecration by the profession of the evangelical counsels and that would identify its scope for development, has indicated the desirability of determining its future role better, as established in canon 579 of the cic, by consulting the opinion of this Congregation before proceeding with the establishment of a new diocesan Institute. Therefore, in accordance with the view of the Pontifical Council for Legislative Texts, the Holy Father Pope Francis at the Audience accorded to the undersigned Secretary of State on 4 April 2016, has set forth that prior consultation with the Holy See is to be understood as necessary *ad validitatem* before establishing a diocesan Institute of consecrated life, otherwise decree of establishment

9 Even though the amount of the deposit continues to increase (1) through (9) can be found in Sharon Holland, "New Institutes, Mergers and Suppression," 39–41 in *Procedural Handbook for Institutes of Consecrated Life and Societies of Apostolic Life* by M. Joyce, C. Darcy, R. Kaslyn and T. Sullivan (Washington, DC: Canon Law Society of America, 2001) ; L. Jarrell and D. Ward, "Procedures for Establishing an Institute/Society," 5–6 in *Procedures and Documents for Canonical and Civil Administration* (Silver Springs, MD: Legal Resource Center for Religious, 2007); and E. Jaramillo, *Evolving Into a Vibrant Religious Institute*, (Maitland, FL: Xulon Press, 2014) 38-39.

> of this said Institute. The present Rescript will be promulgated by way of publication in *L'Osservatore Romano*, and will enter into force, on 1 June 2016, and subsequently be published in the *Acta Apostolicae Sedis*. From the Vatican, Cardinal Pietro Parolin, Secretary of State.[10]

While it is encouraging that you have positive feedback from several officials in Rome, it does not appear that the various requirements have been met. From experience, this author can attest to the fact that putting together this package in order to obtain the *nihil obstat* is not an easy task. Great care must be taken regarding the various requirements in order to prevent delays and exchange of letters. The testimonial letter from the bishop(s) stands out as very significant. The matters he must address describe concisely the important issues for founders and bishops in founding and guiding a new institute. I encourage you to seek help from a canonist.

Eileen Jaramillo, DMin, JCL

10 Secretary of State, Rescript ex audientia SS.mi pertinens ad canonem 579 Codicis Iuris Canonicis de Dioecesanis Institutis erigendis, May 11, 2016: AAS (2016) 696. English Translation: http://www.vatican.va/roman_curia/secretariat_state/parolin/2016/documents/rc_seg-st_20160511_parolin-rescritto-can579cdc_en.html, accessed February 2019.

Canons 934 §1, 2°-§2; 1226; 1228-1229

The Meaning of "Private" in "Private Chapel"

A pastor who requested and received permission from the Vicar General of his archdiocese to have a private chapel in his rectory (cf. can. 1226) and to celebrate Mass there (cf. can. 1228) wonders the exact meaning of "private," asking whether it means that, since only he will use the chapel, he may forego certain canonical and liturgical requirements to which he must adhere in his parish church.

Opinion

The word "private" here has a distinct meaning as observed in Can. 1226 of the 1983 Code of Canon Law: "By the term private chapel is understood a place for divine worship designated by permission of the local ordinary for the benefit of one or more physical persons."

The term *private chapel* is new to the present Code and corresponds to the "private or domestic oratory" mentioned in can. 1188 §2, 3° of the 1917 Code of Canon Law.

Can. 1228 asserts: "Without prejudice to the prescript of can. 1227, the permission of the local ordinary is required for Mass or other sacred celebrations to take place in any private chapel."

And what is also possible, per Can. 934 §1, 2°: "The Most Holy Eucharist: can be reserved in the chapel of the bishop and, with the permission of the local ordinary, in other churches, oratories, and chapels.

The pastor in question currently has a private chapel in his rectory and permission to celebrate Mass there. He may now request permission for the reservation of the Most Blessed Sacrament.

Can. 1229 declares: "It is fitting for oratories and private chapels to be blessed according to the rite prescribed in the liturgical books. They must, however, be reserved for divine worship alone and free from all domestic uses." Unlike churches that are dedicated, private chapels may be blessed.

Clearly, "private" signifies the locus for divine worship. The "Mass and other sacred celebrations" (can. 1228) are public worship even if only the pastor is present. Can. 837 §1 specifies: "Liturgical actions are not private actions but celebrations of the church itself which is *the sacrament of unity*, that is, a holy people gathered and ordered under the bishops. Liturgical actions therefore belong to the whole body of the church and manifest and affect it: they touch its individual members in different ways, however, according to the diversity of orders, functions, and actual participation."

Nothing is foreseen in canon or liturgical law that the normative requirements for Mass and other sacred ceremonies are to be relaxed in a private chapel over against a parish church. During the celebration of the Mass, for example, legitimate options expressed in *The Roman Missal*, may be exercised in the private chapel just as in wherever the Mass is celebrated. Reverence for and care in maintaining the Most Blessed Sacrament, the altar, the tabernacle, etc., are rightly expected wherever the Mass is celebrated and the Most Holy Eucharist is reserved.

Rev. Msgr. Charles M. Mangan, JCL

Canon 967, §2

The Faculty of Hearing the Confessions of Any of the Faithful Everywhere (*Ubique*)

I am a priest-member of a society of apostolic life with the faculty of hearing confessions habitually granted by a diocesan bishop. What is required in order for me to exercise that faculty everywhere both validly and licitly?

Opinion

The first paragraph of canon 967 establishes that, in addition to the Roman Pontiff, cardinals and bishops enjoy the faculty of hearing confessions habitually of any of the Christian faithful everywhere (*ubique*) by the law itself.[1] The second paragraph of canon 967 establishes that this same faculty is enjoyed by three distinct groups of priests:

> Those who possess the faculty of hearing confessions habitually, whether [1] by virtue of office or [2] by virtue of the grant of an ordinary of the place of incardination or [3] of the place in which they have a domicile, can exercise that faculty everywhere [*ubique*] unless the local ordinary has denied it in a particular case, without prejudice to the prescripts of can. 974, §§2 and 3.[2]

The third paragraph of canon 967 concerns the faculty of hearing the confessions only of "members and others living day and night in the house of [an] institute or society," and as such falls outside of the scope of this opinion. This opinion, therefore, will treat the three distinct groups of priests who enjoy the *ubique* faculty specified by canon 967 §2.

The first group is comprised of those priests who enjoy the faculty of hearing confessions habitually by virtue of office—namely:

1. local ordinaries (c. 968, §1)
    b. prelates equivalent in law to a diocesan bishop (cc. 368 and 381, §2)

1 CIC/1983, c. 967, §1. "Praeter Romanum Pontificem, facultate christifidelium ubique terrarum confessiones excipiendi ipso iure gaudent Cardinales; itemque Episcopi, qui eadem et licite ubique utuntur, nisi Episcopus dioecesanus in casu particulari renuerit."

2 Ibid., §2.

iii. territorial prelates
iv. territorial abbots
v. vicars and prefects apostolic
vi. apostolic administrators of stably erected apostolic administrations

b. those who govern an impeded or vacant see (cc. 413; 419; 421)
c. vicars general and episcopal vicars (134, §1)
d. military ordinaries
e. ordinaries of personal ordinariates

2. canons penitentiary (c. 968, §1)

3. pastors (parochi) (ibid.)

4. those who take the place of pastors (ibid.)

a. when the parish becomes vacant or the pastor is impeded
ii. parochial administrators (c. 540, §1)
iii. the parochial vicar senior by appointment before appointment of a parochial administrator (c. 541, §1)

b. priests to whom the pastoral care of a parish is entrusted in solidum (cc. 542-543)
c. a priest provided with the faculties of a pastor who directs a vacant parish (c. 517, §2)

5. chaplains[3] (c. 566, §1)

Since each of these offices (with the possible exception of chaplain) is clearly defined in law, this first category presents no particular difficulties of interpretation. It is important to note, however, that major superiors of institutes or societies are not *local* ordinaries, nor do they enjoy the *ubique* faculty by virtue of office.

The second group is comprised of those priests who enjoy the faculty of hearing confessions habitually by virtue of a grant from an ordinary of the place where they are incardinated (c. 967, §2). The word "place" is very important

3 "According to the norm of c. 967, §2, the faculty of hearing confessions conceded to the chaplain *vi officii* is able to be exercised everywhere (*ubique*), unless, in a particular case, the local ordinary has forbidden it." Luigi Chiappetta, *Il Codice di diritto canonico: Commento giuridico-pastorale*, 3rd ed. (Bologna: Edizione Dehoniane Bologna, 2011), 1: 688; translation my own. "In relation to the faculty of hearing the confession of the faithful entrusted to his care, we are dealing with one of the habitual faculties that c. 132, §1 talks about which corresponds to the chaplain by virtue of office and that can be exercised with the breadth provided in c. 967, §2." Eloy Tejero, in *Exegetical Commentary on the Code of Canon Law*, ed. Ernest Lagges Caparros, vol. II/2 (Montréal: Wilson & Lafleur, 2004), p. 1434. "A priest is granted by this canon *ipso iure* the faculty to hear confession for all the faithful anywhere in the world: [...] in virtue of an office held ... e.g., canon penitentiary, pastor, chaplain [...]." William H. Woestman, *Sacraments: Initiation, Penance, Anointing of the Sick: Commentary on Canons 840-1007*, 3rd ed. (Ottawa: Faculty of Canon Law, Saint Paul University, 2004), p. 244.

here, since this kind of faculty can only be granted by a *local* ordinary (c. 969, §1); again, major superiors of institutes or societies are not similarly competent (c. 969, §2). This is the usual way for diocesan priests who do not enjoy the *ubique* faculty by virtue of office to obtain it.

The third group is comprised of those priests who enjoy the faculty of hearing confessions habitually by virtue of a grant from an ordinary of the place where they have acquired domicile (c. 967, §2). Domicile may be acquired in three ways. The first two ways are common to all of the Christian faithful: "Domicile is acquired by that residence within the territory of a certain parish or at least of a diocese, which either [1] is joined with the intention of remaining there permanently unless called away or [2] has been protracted for five complete years" (c. 102, §1).

The following two examples illustrate this distinction. In the first place, consider a priest who retires to a diocese in which he is not incardinated, having every intention of remaining there until his death. In that case, he acquires domicile from the first day of taking up residence. If he were to receive the faculty of hearing confessions habitually from a local ordinary of that diocese, he could exercise it everywhere by virtue of canon 967, §2. Secondly, consider a priest who begins to minister in a neighboring diocese on a temporary basis.

> He knows [...] that sooner or later he will be moved [outside of the diocese]: he does not acquire domicile from the beginning, because, while waiting for the transfer [...], he neither has nor is able to have the intention of remaining indefinitely in that [diocese]. He will acquire domicile only after five years of actual residence.[4]

After having acquired domicile, he, too, would enjoy the *ubique* faculty.

The third way of acquiring domicile is unique to members of institutes or societies, who, in addition to the two ways mentioned above, also "acquire a domicile in the place where the house to which they are attached is located" (c. 103). By "house" here is meant any canonically erected permanent residence (abbey, monastery, convent, priory, house, etc.). This domicile may helpfully be thought of as a member's "legal address." It is rather common for a member who does not actually reside at his "legal address" to obtain two domiciles—one according to canon 102, §1, and another according to canon 103.[5]

---

4 Chiappetta, *Commento*, 1: 123-124; translation my own.

5 See ibid., 1:125; Amadeo de Fuenmayer, in *Exegetical Commentary on the Code of Canon Law*, ed. Ernest Lagges Caparros, vol. I (Montréal: Wilson & Lafleur, 2004), p. 712.

The principal practical difficulty arises when a priest who enjoys the faculty of hearing confessions habitually *only* by virtue of a grant from an ordinary of a diocese where he is not domiciled is called upon to minister outside of that diocese. That is to say, the priest in question is neither in possession of a canonical office to which this faculty is attached by law, nor is he incardinated there, nor is he attached to a canonically erected house there. Outside of cases involving the danger of death (c. 976), such a priest absolves validly and licitly *only within the jurisdiction of the ordinary who granted the faculty*. Such a situation can be remedied, however, by asking an ordinary of the place of domicile also to grant the faculty of hearing confessions habitually.[6] Lacking such a grant—as tedious as it may seem—the priest must obtain an additional faculty of hearing confessions from an ordinary of each diocese to which he is sent to minister.

What happens, then, when a priest who erroneously thinks he enjoys the *ubique* faculty attempts to absolve a penitent outside of his proper jurisdiction? While obviously not applicable to all situations, in cases of common error or positive and probable doubt *de iure* or *de facto*, the Church herself supplies the necessary faculty (c. 144).[7]

Rev. Brian T. Austin, FSSP, JCL

6 See Pontifical Commission *Ecclesia Dei*, private letter concerning the faculty of hearing confessions *ubique terrarum*, Prot. No. 153/2009, 6 May 2010.

7 While a treatment of common error is beyond the scope of this opinion, see John M. Huels, "The Supply of the Faculty to Confirm in Common Error," *Studia canonica* 40 (2006): pp. 299-301, 327-328. For a consideration of the case where a priest knowingly provokes common error, see ibid., pp. 342-343.

Canon 1336, 1369, and 1399

Right of the Bishop to Impose a Penalty by Extrajudicial Decree

For offences such as maligning the pope, or for child safeguarding reasons, can a bishop stop lay members of the faithful from attending mass in a particular community and insist they attend another mass?

Opinion

A member of an ethnic community produced a mockumentary loaded on YouTube arguing that the world is controlled by corporates who use things like religion to control people. In the video the pope is described as one of the world's richest men who does not care about the poor.

The ethnic community were offended, and described the member as a spy. They vehemently opposed the member and his wife coming to their ethnic community mass. They asked the bishop to force them to attend mass elsewhere.

Canon 1369 states:

> A person who in a public show or speech, in published writing, or in other uses of the instruments of social communication utters blasphemy, gravely injures good morals, expresses insults, or excites hatred or contempt against religion or the Church is to be punished with a just penalty.

The member of the ethnic community refused to remove his mockumentary from YouTube and submitted it for an award in an international competition. He gave interviews in the secular media justifying what he had done.

Canon 1336 states:

> §1. In addition to other penalties which the law may have established, the following are expiatory penalties which can affect an offender either perpetually, for a prescribed time, or for an indeterminate time:
>
> No. 1. a prohibition or an order concerning residence in a certain place or territory;

No. 2. privation of a power, office, function, right, privilege, faculty, favor, title, or insignia, even merely honorary;

No. 3. a prohibition against exercising those things listed under n. 2, or a prohibition against exercising them in a certain place or outside a certain place; these prohibitions are never under pain of nullity;

The Congresso of the Signatura decreed in a parallel case involving a disruptive parishioner that a bishop can impose lawfully a penal decree on a lay member of Christ's faithful. A bishop had given a penal precept to a parishioner who was disturbing liturgical celebrations in a parish and she had appealed the decision to the Apostolic Signatura.

Canon 1371 states:

The following are to be punished with a just penalty:

No. 1. in addition to the case mentioned in canon 1364 §1, a person who teaches a doctrine condemned by the Roman Pontiff or an ecumenical council or who obstinately rejects the doctrine mentioned in canon 750, §2 or in canon 752 and who does not retract after having been admonished by the Apostolic See or an ordinary;

No. 2. a person who otherwise does not obey a legitimate precept or prohibition of the Apostolic See, an ordinary, or a superior and who persists in disobedience after a warning.

The Congresso of the Apostolic Signatura decreed 30 October 1990:

That according to the norm of canon 1371 no 2, one who does not comply with a legitimately prescribing ordinary or who obstinately persists in disobedience after a warning can be punished with a just penalty;

That, taking canon 1358 §1 together with 1336 §1, penalties imposed for a predetermined time are to be considered expiatory;

That the prohibition to enter a certain church or to participate in liturgical celebration is an expiatory penalty to be joined to those which are articulated in canon 1336 §1, no. 3.

Admitting that the same penalty is aptly called by the name taken from the law itself, namely a prohibition (prohibition), while nothing forbids it from being called, although less precisely, the equivalent of an "interdict" (*interdictum*).

When a bishop is imposing a penalty by extrajudicial decree, he must weigh the matter, including proofs and arguments, with two assessors.

> Canon 1720. If the ordinary thinks that the matter must proceed by way of extrajudicial decree:
>
> No. 1. he is to inform the accused of the accusation and the proofs, giving an opportunity for self-defense, unless the accused neglected to appear after being properly summoned;
>
> No. 2. he is to weigh carefully all the proofs and arguments with two assessors;
>
> No. 3. if the delict is certainly established and a criminal action is not extinguished, he is to issue a decree according to the norm of canons 1342-1350, setting forth the reasons in law and in fact at least briefly.

The chaplain and the ethnic community did not want disturbances or upset at the ethnic community celebrations of the Eucharist caused by the presence of the member who had maligned the pope. Therefore, the diocesan bishop, following correct procedures, can prohibit participation in divine worship at that particular ethnic community mass according to the norms of canon 1336, §1, no. 3 by issuing an extrajudicial decree for a just cause (canon 1720). The bishop could instruct the member to attend Sunday mass at another ethnic community or parish mass.

In the second case, a lay member of the faithful has been convicted in a civil court of the crime of sexual abuse of a minor. After he came out of prison, parents objected to him being at a mass where there were many children present. Sexual abuse by a layperson was not specifically legislated as a crime according to the 1983 Code. However, canon 1399 encompasses the case because it includes the external violation of a divine law including the sixth commandment.

> Canon 1399. In addition to the cases established here or in other laws, the external violation of a divine or canonical law can be punished by a just penalty only when the special gravity of the violation demands punishment and there is an urgent need to prevent or repair scandals.

Again the bishop can proceed by using an extrajudicial decree, following correct procedures, weighing the matter, including proofs and arguments, with two assessors.

Consequently, a bishop could prohibit the lay member of the faithful from attending Sunday mass where many children are present. The bishop could require him to attend mass at a religious community early in the morning when children would only be in the congregation on rare occasions.

Rev. Msgr. Brendan P. Daly, JCD

Contributors

Rev. Brian T. Austin, FSSP, JCL is the Assistant Administrator of the Oratory of Saints Philomena and Cecilia in the Archdiocese of Indianapolis, Indiana.

Very Rev. Patrick Cooney, OSB, JCL, is the Judicial Vicar for the Diocese of Owensboro, Kentucky.

Rev. Msgr. Brendan P. Daly, JCD, is Judicial Vicar for the Tribunal of the Catholic Church in New Zealand and a lecturer in canon law at Good Shepherd College.

Sr. Sharon Euart, RSM, JCD, is the Executive Director of the Resource Center for Religious Institutes in Silver Spring, Maryland.

Dr. Eileen C. Jaramillo, DMin, JCL, is a Professor of Canon Law at Siena Heights University in Adrian, Michigan, and a Canonical Consultant in Lansing, Michigan.

Rev. Msgr. Charles M. Mangan, JCL, is the Vicar for Consecrated Life for the Diocese of Sioux Falls, South Dakota.

Donna Miller, JD, JCL, is the Executive Coordinator of the Canon Law Society of America.

Meg Romano-Hogan, JCL, is the Director of Pastoral Services for Marriage and Family Life, St. Thomas Auinas Church, Dallas, TX.

Rev. Msgr. John Renken, JCD, is the Dean of the Faculty of Canon Law at Saint Paul University, Ottawa, Ontario, Canada.

Rev. Msgr. Michael A. Souckar, JCD, is the Adjutant Judicial Vicar for the Archdiocese of Miami, Florida, and Pastor of St. Andrew Catholic Church in Coral Springs, Florida.

Therese Guerin Sullivan, SP, JCL is a Sister of Providence of St. Mary-of-the-Woods, Indiana.

Made in the USA
Monee, IL
14 September 2026

62974514R00036